COCREATOR I AM

GOD IN ME Y I IN GOD

Marcos Cervantes Janssen

LETRA ROJA

I AM COCREATOR

God in me
Y
I in God

By: Marcos Cervantes Janssen

INDEX:

FOREWORD:

This writing is not religious in any way, what I expose is a reality, in the psychological and social area that is based on real facts, of our life history. I deal with the theme of God in its pure and complete sense of EXISTENTIAL totality , without dogmas or doctrines.

Actually we all are co-creators conscious and unconscious of existing, everything that is created and destroyed, exists within the continuous transformation of all coexisting events. The great opportunity to be a Co-Creator is through the conscious state of our awakened mind. Let's remember that an awakened mind, faces reality, is a flow directed by each conscious and unconscious individual, who with their actions, shapes with the past in the present, a constant future. We will see how each time and phase of our history entails its different degrees of awareness, generation and acceptance of reality in progress, IT IS WHAT IT IS, it is presented at each moment of our time, learning as a method of natural evolution in each being that live awake to the changes made within the collective historical flow, so we will find our originality within a fraternal scheme of universal integration.

INTENTION:

The intention is a mental energy, fundamental for creation, the intention is formed in the mind; They are thoughts with structures and data which make up a potentiality to be realized.

Imagination, dreams and projects are intentions; These, the more details and structural calculations conform, the intentional thought, takes more potential. Our brain with all the data correlated to times and forms, is predisposed to emit signals to all the members of our body, and it is like that of an intention, contained in a thought, made up of experiential data and new designs created by logic, are added to new combination options, thus innovation arises. The intention is the mental growth of an idea, to the degree that by expansive necessity it ceases to be only a psychic energy and through our bodily peripherals it becomes motor action, where the mouth, hands and feet take the first step. in the transformation of intention into action.

As a very simple example, the smile. This comes directly from the mental intention to reveal the internal state of our thoughts, whether spontaneous or by choice.

DECISION:

The decision represents the present of this matter, the decision is the midpoint between the intention and the action, the decision is the so-called floating point, it is in the decision where the choice is executed. This can be conscious and unconscious, generated by reason or by natural instinct. Many times the decision is exercised by learning or collective behavior, responding to group obedience, plus each one of us, we also have the ability to get out of the scheme, and innovate. It is the decision which follows the mathematical flow in an equation, in two ways; projection by average, or reassessment and alteration in its variables, to obtain unbiased results, more if predictable. We can decide to continue a legacy of experience, and stick to a stable projection, or take the logical risk of an improvement in the projection, and intentionally modify the variables to obtain a planned projection result. Thus, it is possible to decide under the prudence of a constant evolution, or cause chaos in the known order to find new horizons in which to innovate in the future, in any case the evolution will continue, it is only a matter of times and forms.

ACTION:

Action is this third phase, where material reality appears. The action is the sum of the intention plus the decision. Action is the energetic outlet of our thoughts, whether conscious or unconscious. An action without intention and without choice is therefore only an attempt without projection or planning, and its result is merely random. A true action thought and developed with time, demonstrates that consciousness is therefore order in chaos. Chaos is the accumulation of necessary components to form a system called order, so we within the universe and each one thinking differently, respond to a natural order for the conformation of this civilization. In the same way, all the particles that coexist within our body seem like a chaos of substances and compounds that, being directed by our mind and the universe, make up our wonderful body and its multiple and precise life processes. We in EXISTENCE and an existential universe that is in us, together with the explainable and the inexplicable, make up the INFINITE ABSOLUTE TOTAL. We are not only part of something bigger, we are part of the ETERNAL and also eternal. Eternal existentially, and in turn biologically, temporary.

REACTION:

The reaction to an action is always expected, more often than not calculated, after the intention, the decision, and the action, the fourth phase is called reaction, this is the transformation resulting from a first intention.

The reaction is already the answer, it is the non-reversible general transformation, so it is to denote the importance of the decision before the action, this leads us to value the decision as the divine exercise of the human being. The whole decides the parameters that surround and shape us, plus the power to choose is particular and personal. The fun thing in life is finding expected reactions, due to having planned the actions, an intelligent intention, and correct decisions, accentuated in more exact actions to obtain the planned or designed reactions, we call this creation. The reaction under our will combined with the natural reaction of the environment, entails a high degree of co-creation, we will always have reactions, created intentionally or by the natural flow of the consequence of the permanent flow, time does not stop, just like that form the creation continues permanently without stopping, to participate consciously is to interact with love to the totality of creation,**COCREAR.**

EVALUATION:

The creation of the absolute is Eternal and constant in its most stable and organized changes in its totality, the ordered chaos. Evaluating is a fundamental part of the transformation, because after each reaction, the evaluation produces a new intention with more precise alignments in each cycle, we call this evolution. To evaluate is known as the full quotient of evolution, to evaluate in our existence, allows us not to repeat aberrant cycles of stagnation again. I will give the magnificent example of the terrestrial rotation around the sun; It seems repetitive but the reality is that the planet earth in each rotation is no longer in the same position in space, its movement is like the figure of a spring, each time it rotates it moves through stellar space, like this In this way, the galaxy in its entirety travels through infinite space, in the universal order, we do not perceive this movement due to the relativity of time, but its speeds and displacement are incredibly enormous. Evaluating is putting situations, intentions, decisions, actions and reactions on a scale to study the processes and learn, evaluating allows us to have the complete picture of the situation, and how creators evolve with creation.

CONFRONTATION:

Once the entire situation and its parts have been evaluated, we confront the possible intentions, so in this way the decision will be made in a mature and wise manner. confronting is often an unwanted and uncomfortable process, since the different parties to be confronted eliminate each other, resulting in an evaluation of equilibrium in search of the optimal advance called evolution. The confrontation of events allows to average the forces and results for a better conformation of the existential future, to confront is to put the truth on the table to make radical decisions in favor of required changes. In social life the comparison is truly uncomfortable but necessary, thanks to the confrontation, relations will be able to clarify everything in question, and it leads to unimaginable agreements due to the lack of mutual knowledge between the affected parties. So the carconfrontation requires personal acceptance for individual development; thus promoting the co-creation of our existential walk, confronting ourselves internally is the way to understand the universe and its evolution processes, through full confrontation. I put for example in the galaxy, the magnetic confrontation and even the impacts, which in turn are necessary.

EVOLUTION:

Evolution is the enveloping action of the collective consciousness of being with being, thus conscious doing, confronted with the decision, allows us to glimpse the paths of growth through conscious co-creation, and the acceptance of belonging to an absolute that in definition eternal evolves under immovable universal laws, but understandable. Thus, knowing our existence and its movement, co-creating means synchronizing our being with everything eternally. Confronting ourselves with our intent to change is the necessary intention to evaluate to achieve the correct decision for life alignment, and constant evolution.

To evolve means to walk in the direction of the existential flow. Evolving is achieved by waking up and accepting the totality that we cohabit, cooperating intelligently and positively to all processes of existence and coexistence, own decision and acceptance of themover collective in favor of a true common good that is called permanent and maintained EVOLUTION. create and leave creating for eternity, it is the integral awakening. Existence awaits our awakening to achieve together the predestined flow of true EVOLUTION. Let's enjoy co-creating and we will evolve without a doubt, let's use our opportunity to live fully to cooperate.

EPILOGUE:

You can write a book, you can also build your house; even better, you can father a child, and you can cultivate this beautiful planet, and in this way you will transform the world. It is here when it is evident that he has the opportunity to be eternal, in his cooperation with existence. The question is: Why shouldn't I take this option in life?

We are part of the whole, and the whole would not be complete or full with our existential absence, for this reason to live asleep is to reject the fullness, the whole is in charge of waking us up since our individual collaboration is required.

I must ensure that many living beings, which do not exercise intention, choice, action, reaction and of course neither evolution, are filling factors for the conformation of the TOTAL plan. unconsciousness is part of the absolute ALL, they are those mysterious zones of existence useful for the Absolute plan of existence, for which reason these unconscious, asleep or complements of existence are irreplaceable and important for our TOTAL existence. The psychological maxim **"IT IS WHAT IT IS"**, defines that reality is absolute and inclusive, but not our temporal perception and understanding.

"LET US LIVE IN HIM AND WITH HIM INSIDE"

This writing is not religious in any way, what I expose is a reality, in the psychological and social area that is based on real facts, of our life history. I deal with the theme of God in its pure and complete sense of EXISTENTIAL totality , without dogmas or doctrines. Actually we all are co-creators conscious and unconscious of existing, everything that is created and destroyed, exists within the continuous transformation of all coexisting events. The great opportunity to be a Co-Creator is through the conscious state of our awakened mind.